THIS EASTER BOOK BELONGS TO

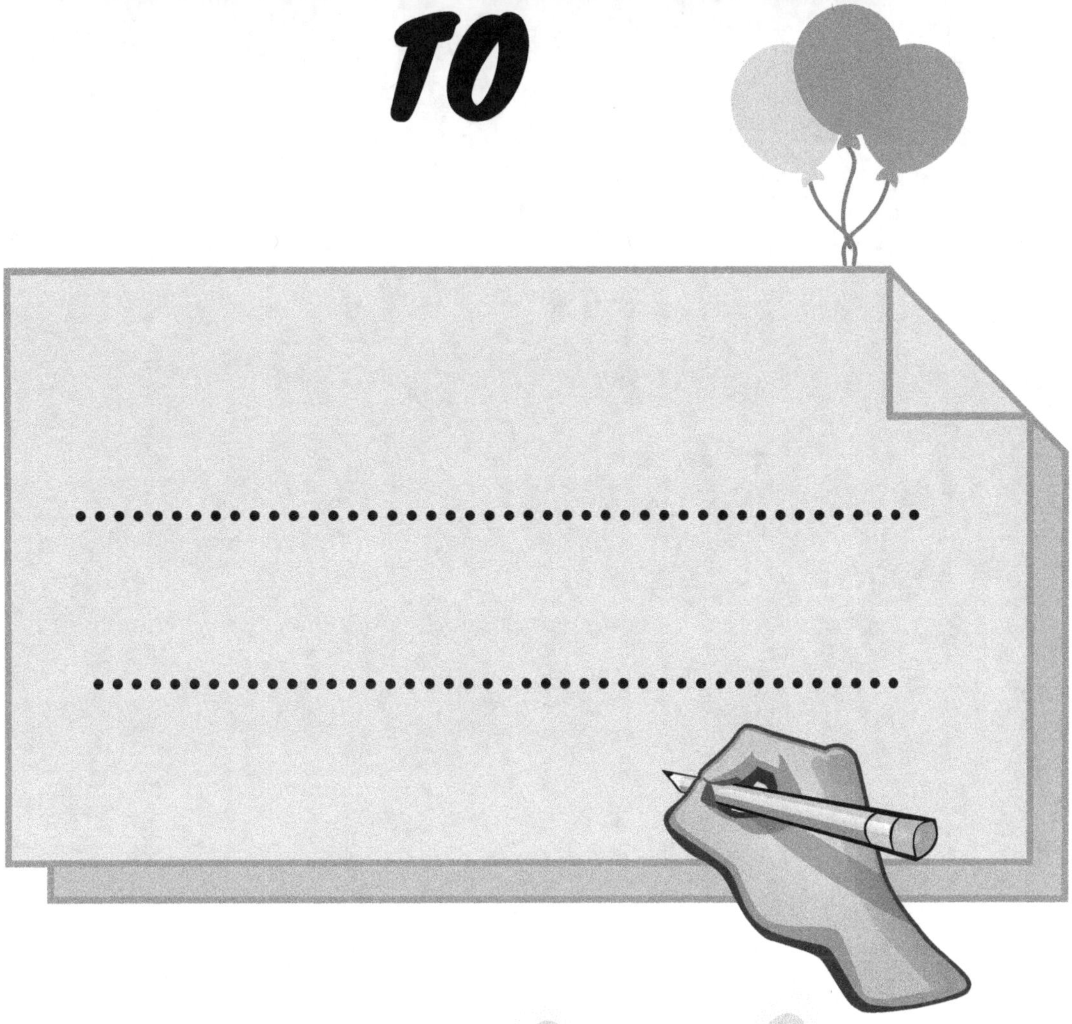

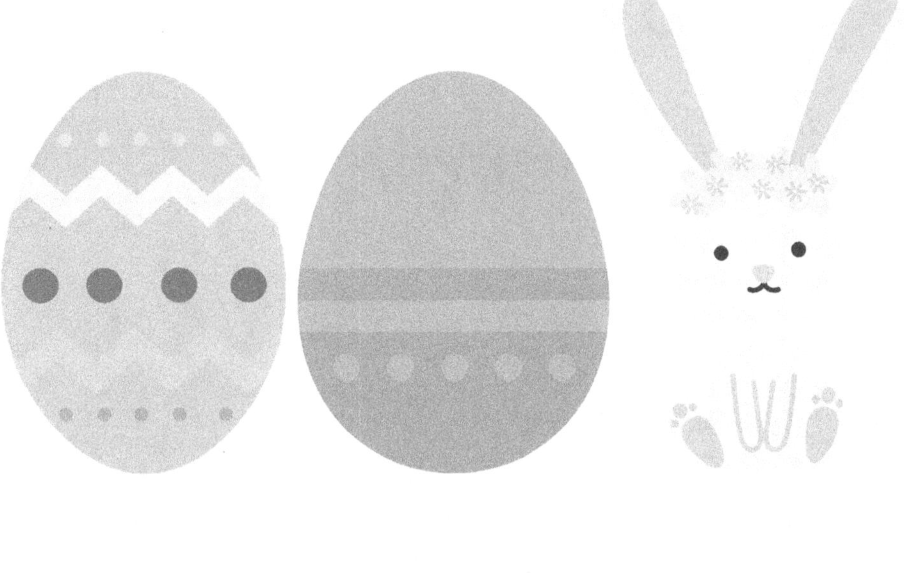

....

....

STEP 1:

Cut out the sheet using trim line.

STEP 2:

Color the picture.

STEP 3:

Carefully cut out the picture using the guide
line.

STEP 4:

Paste on another sheet or hang.
Have fun!

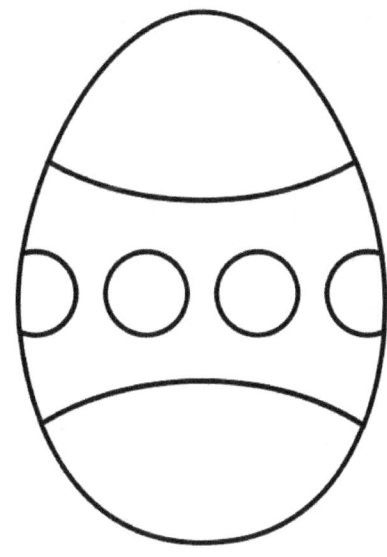

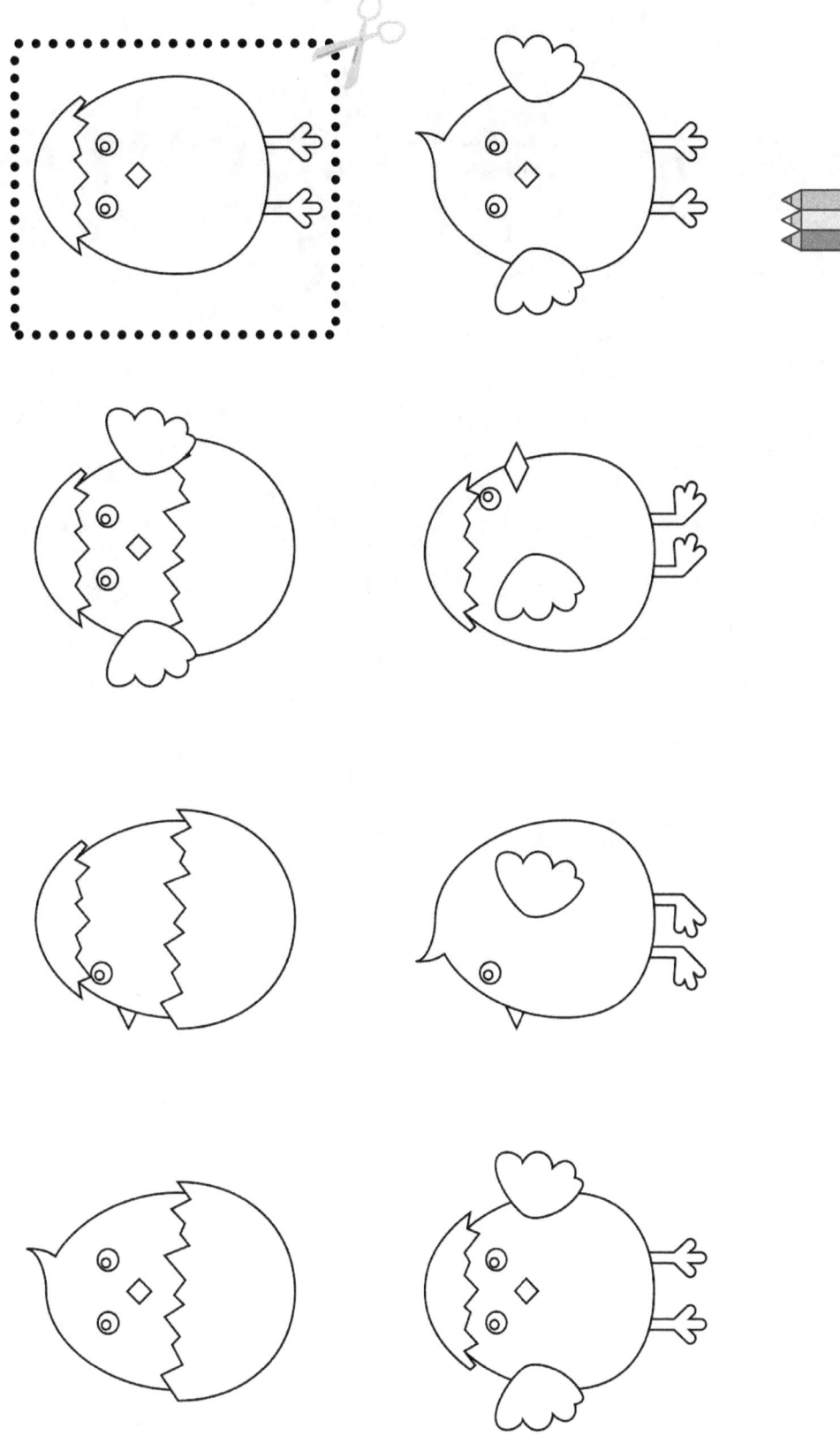

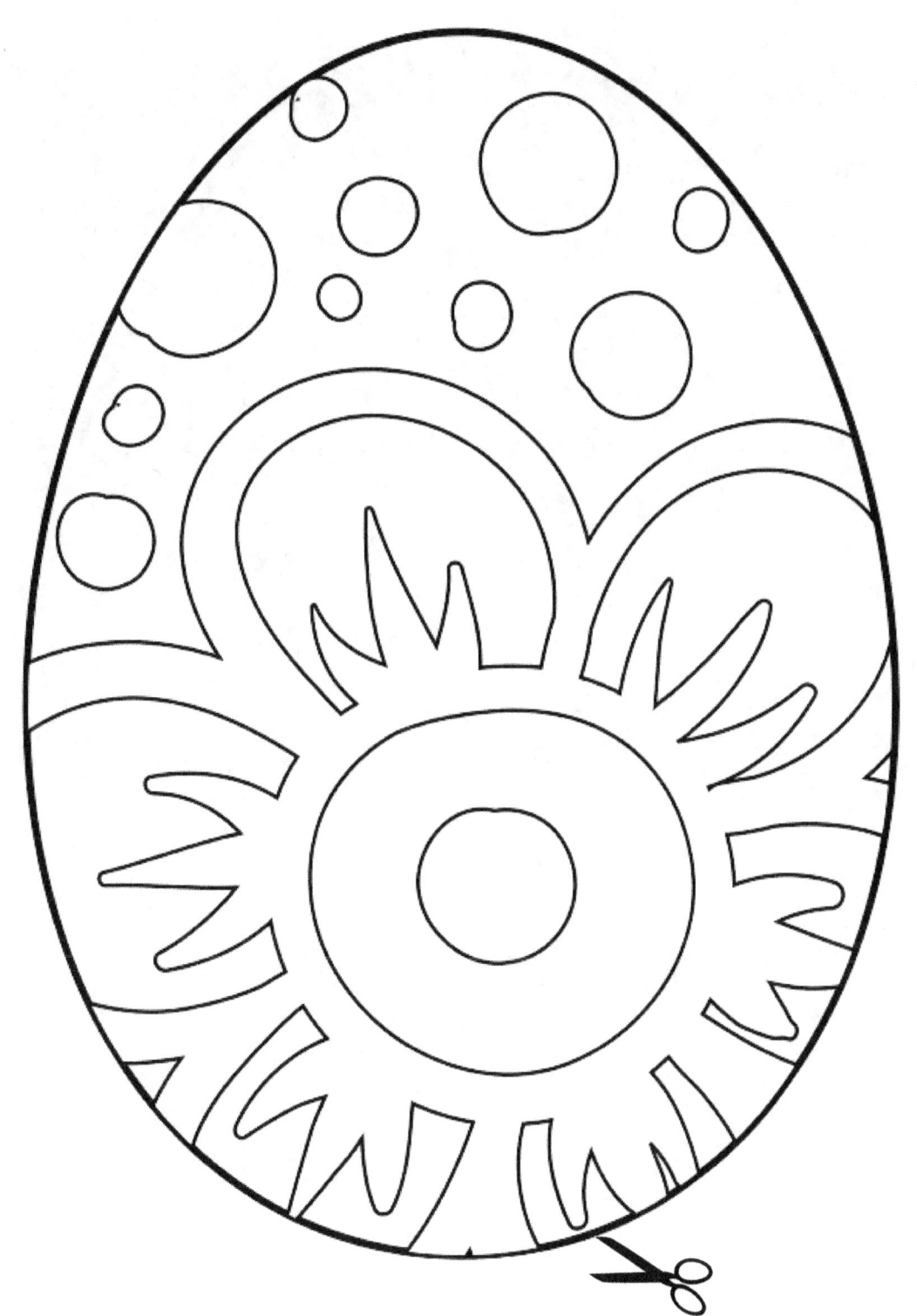

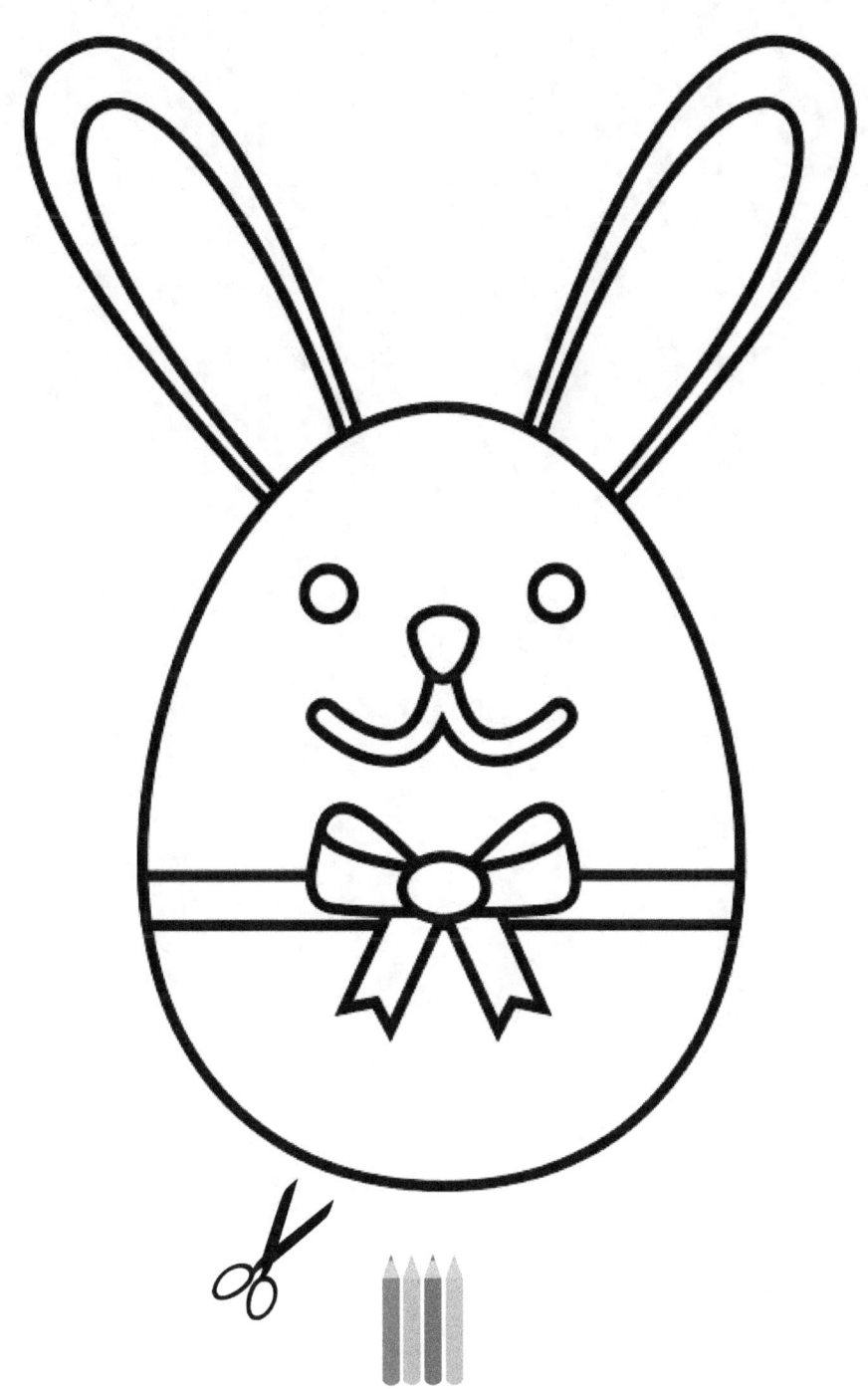

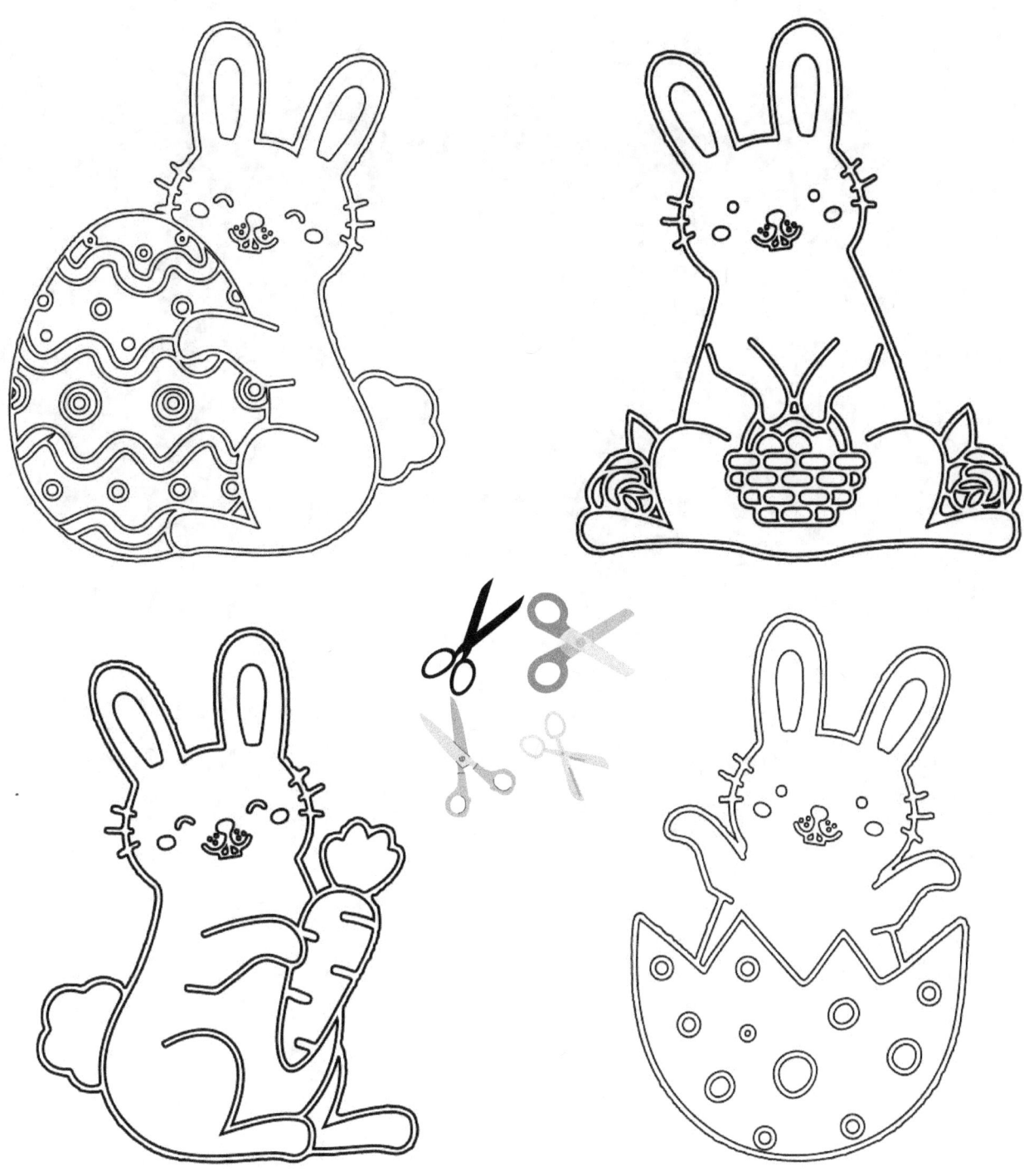

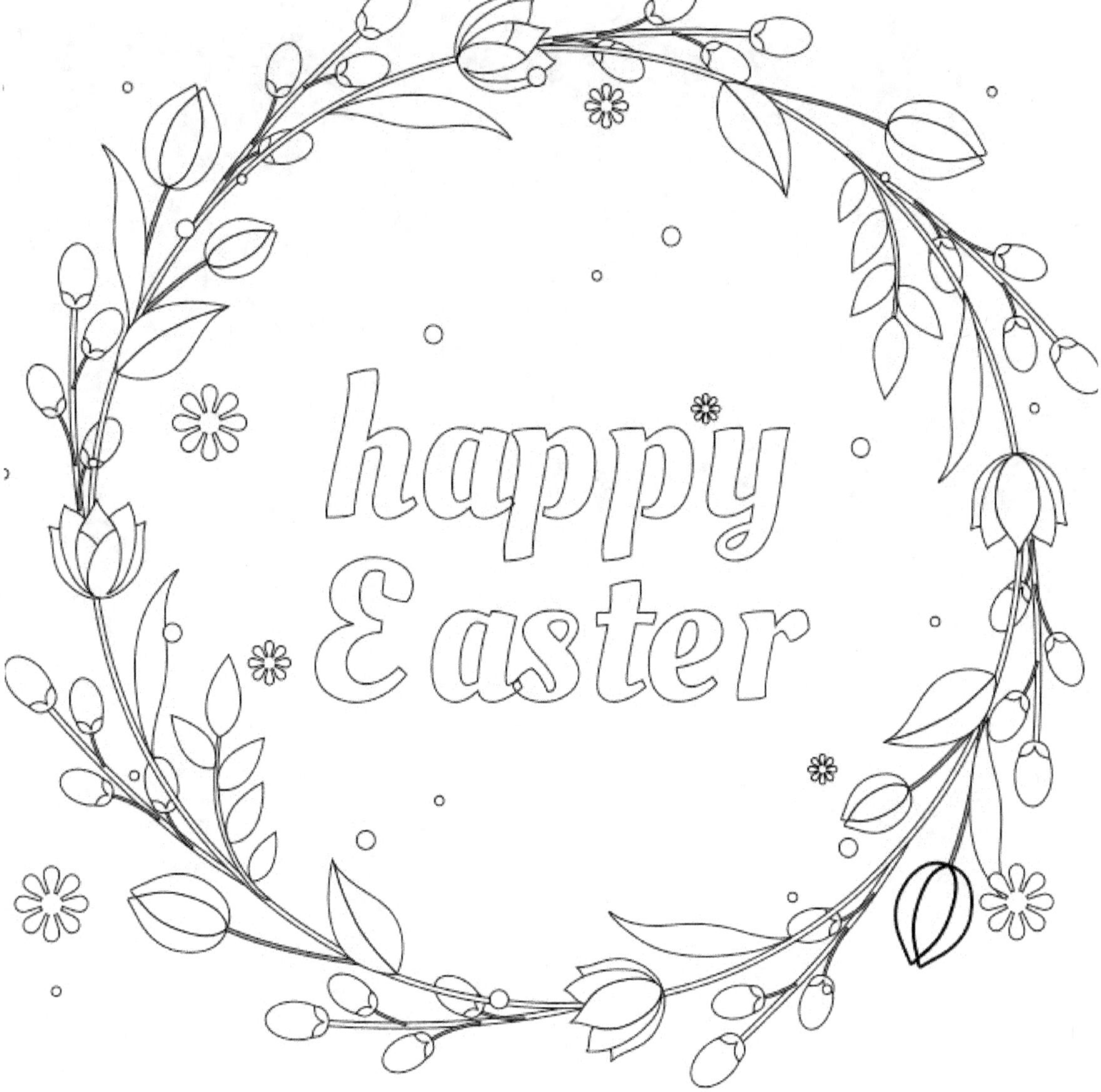

happy
Easter

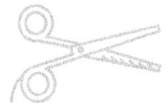

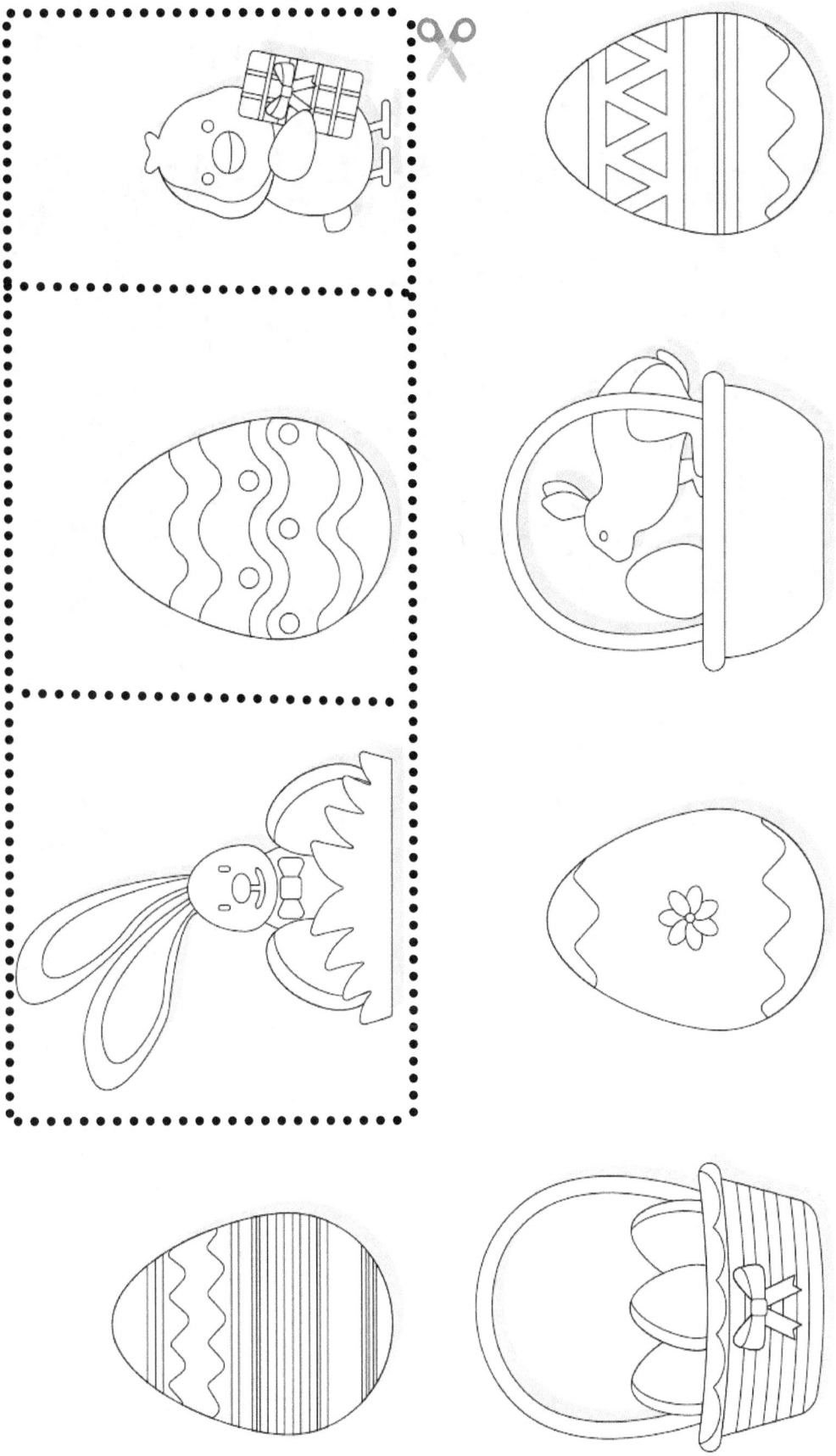

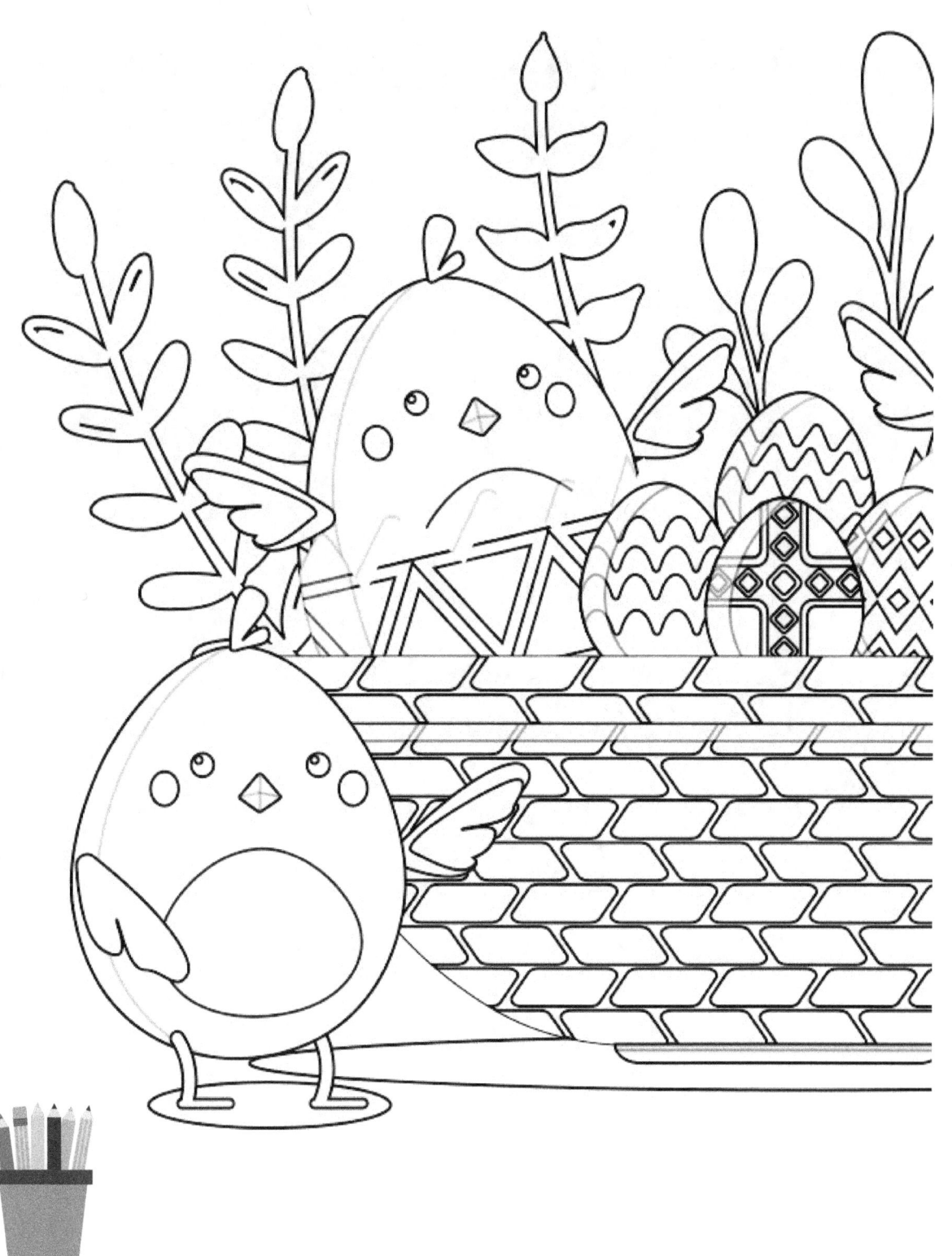

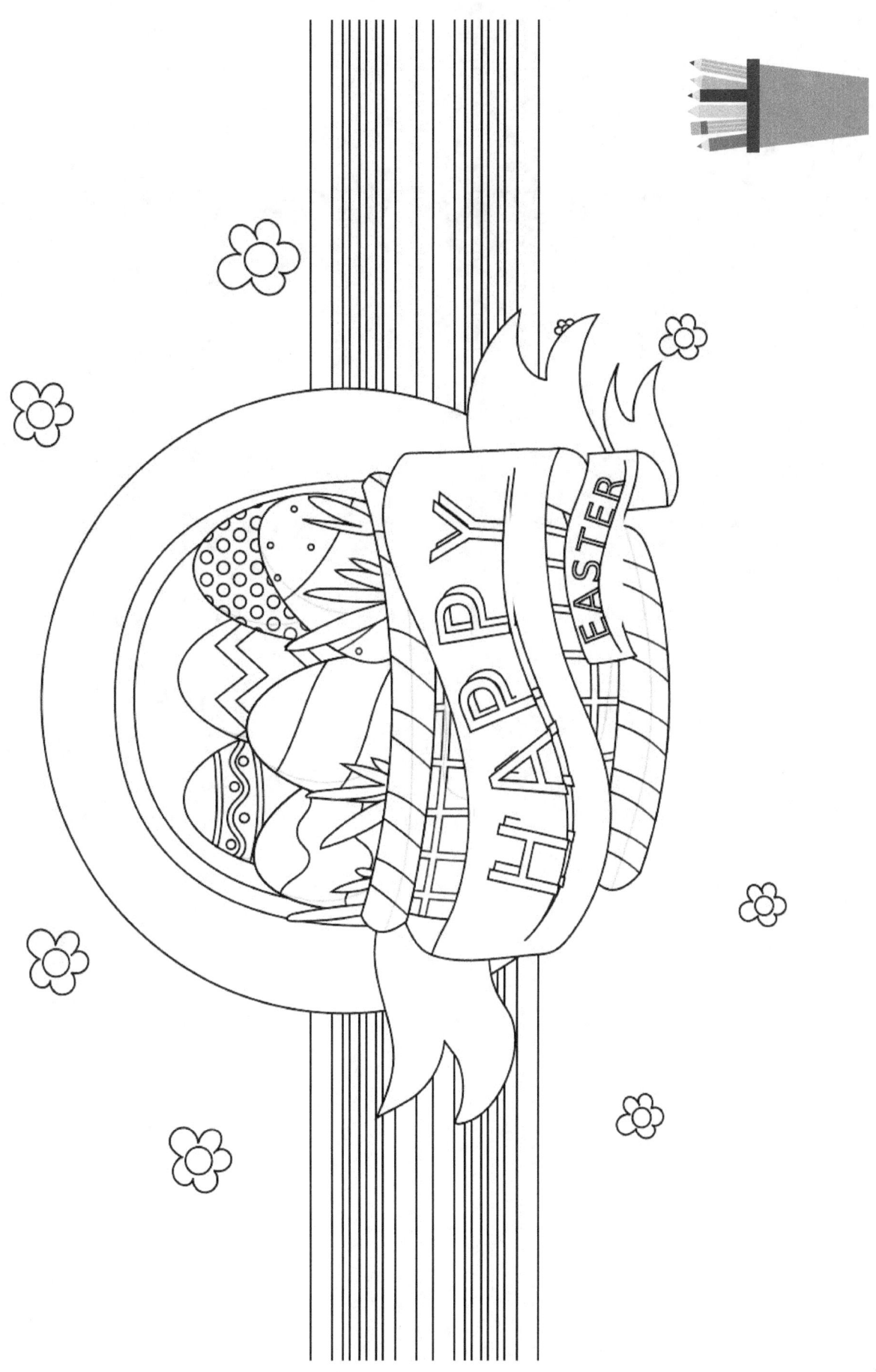

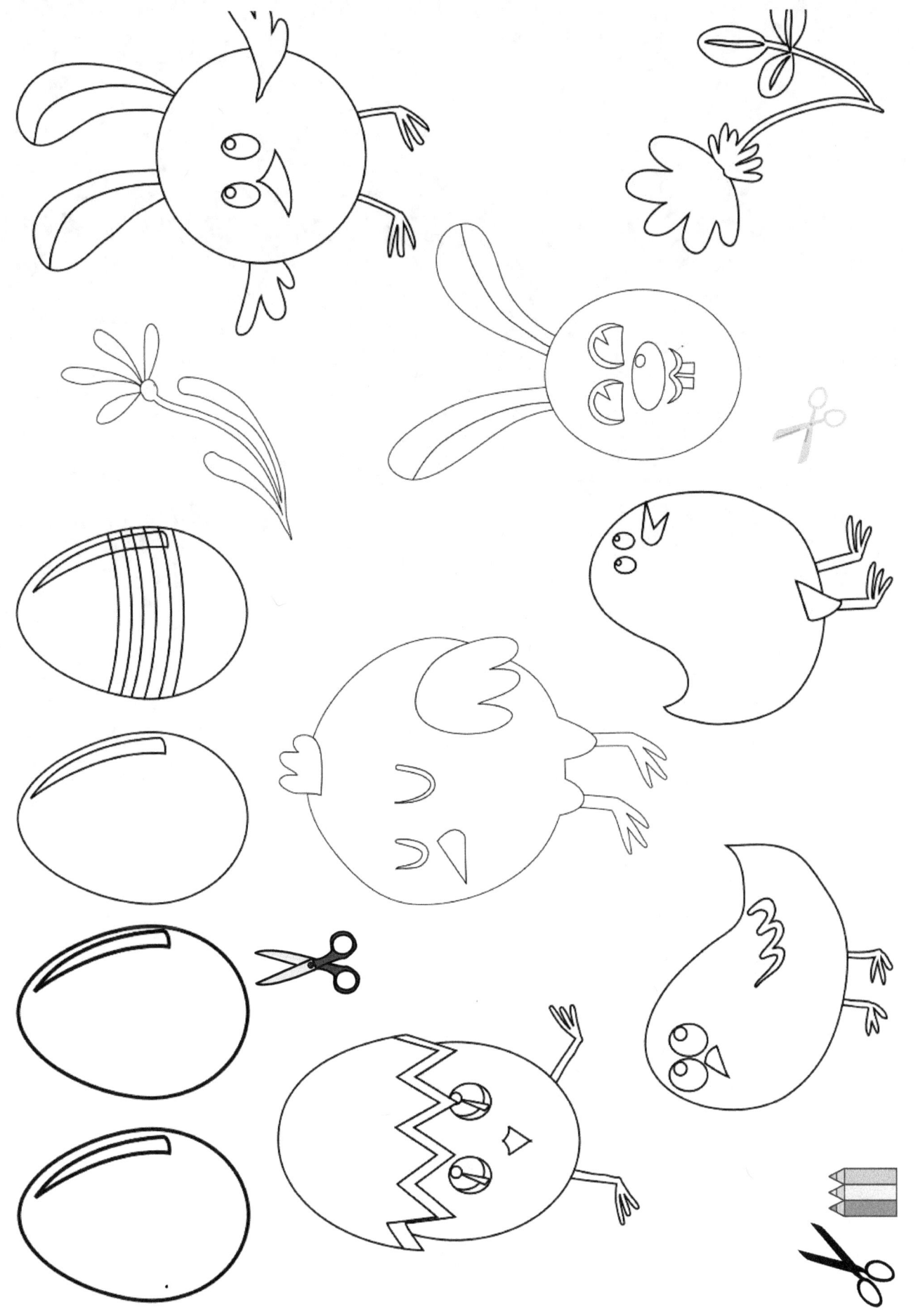

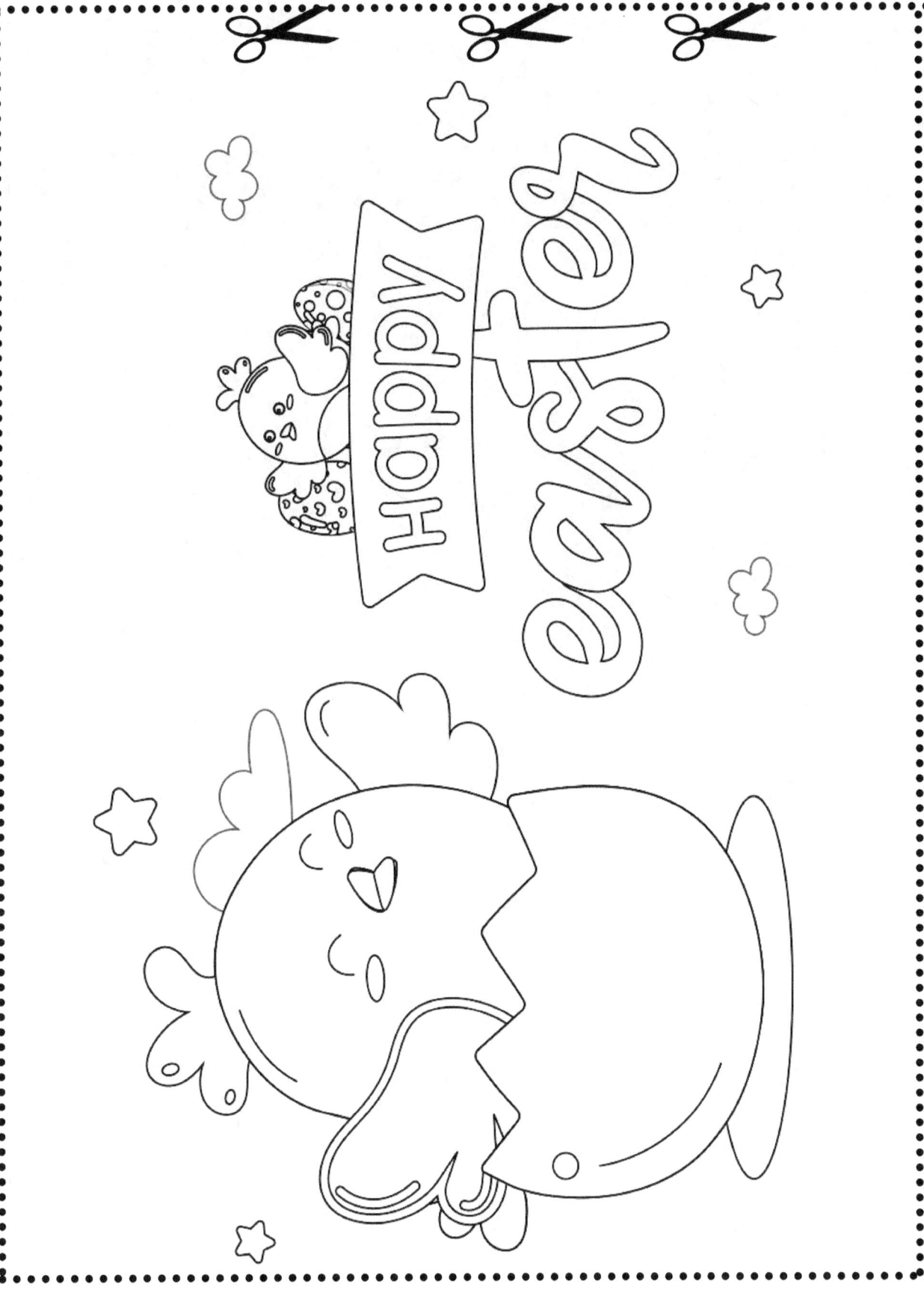

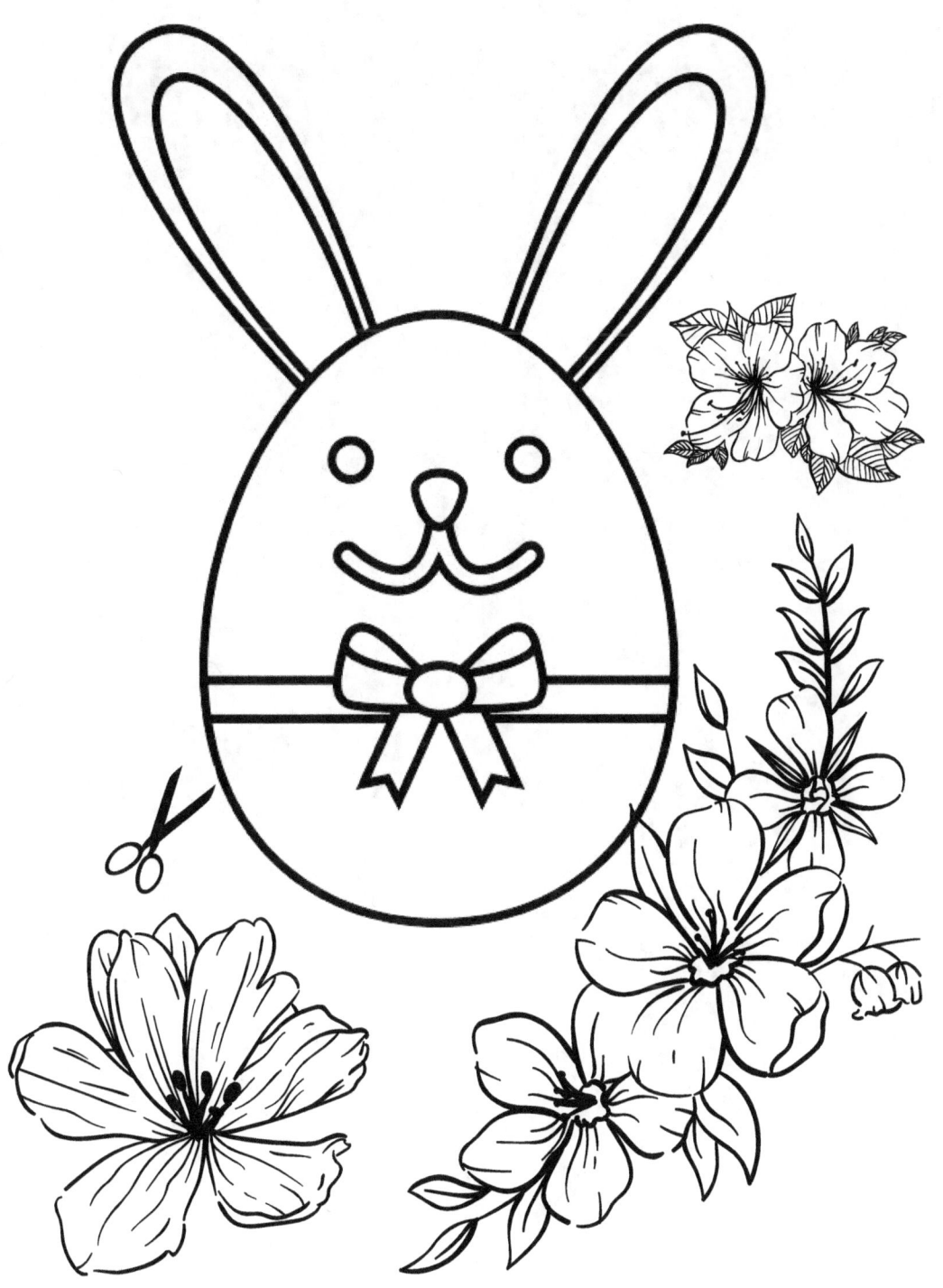

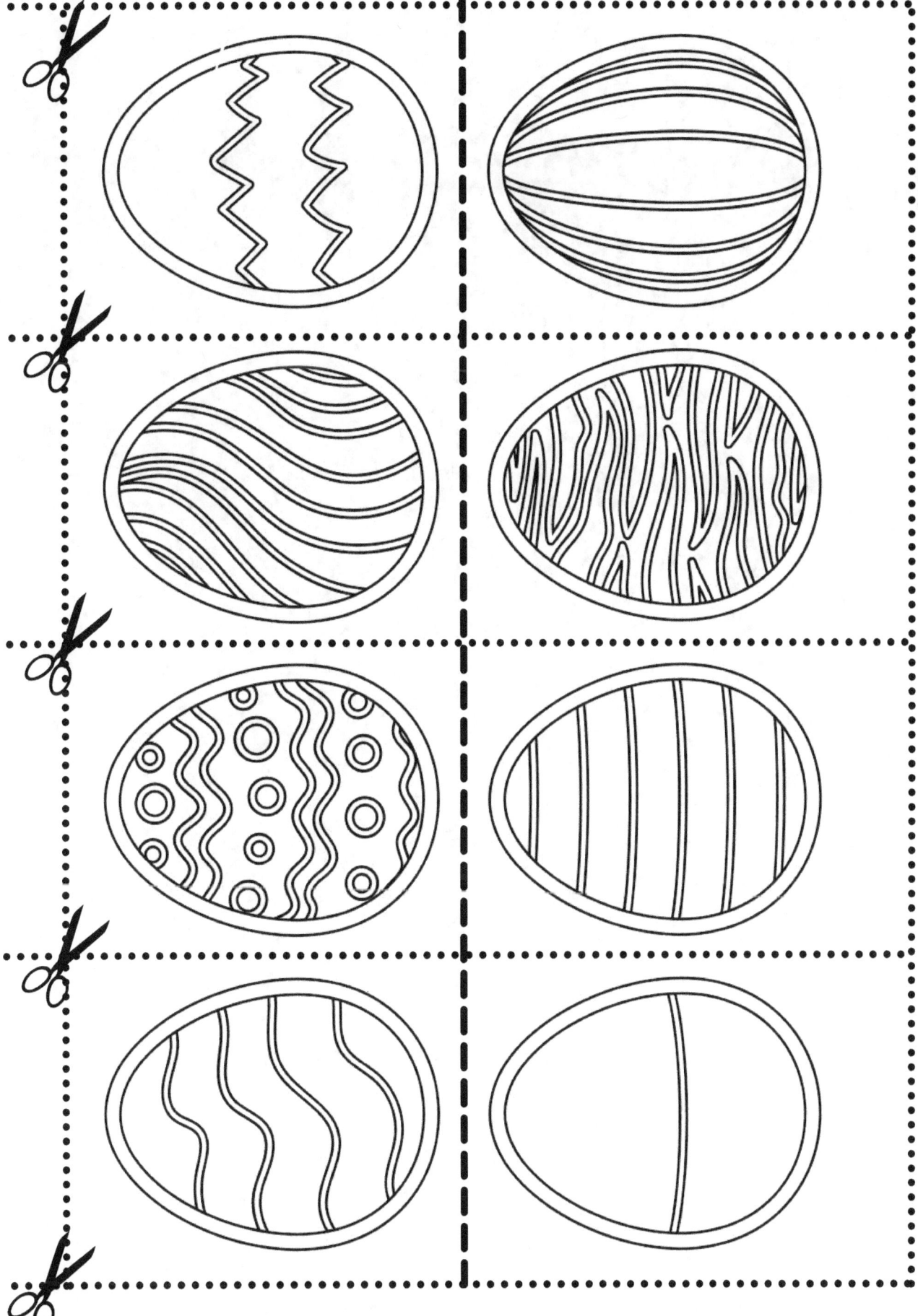

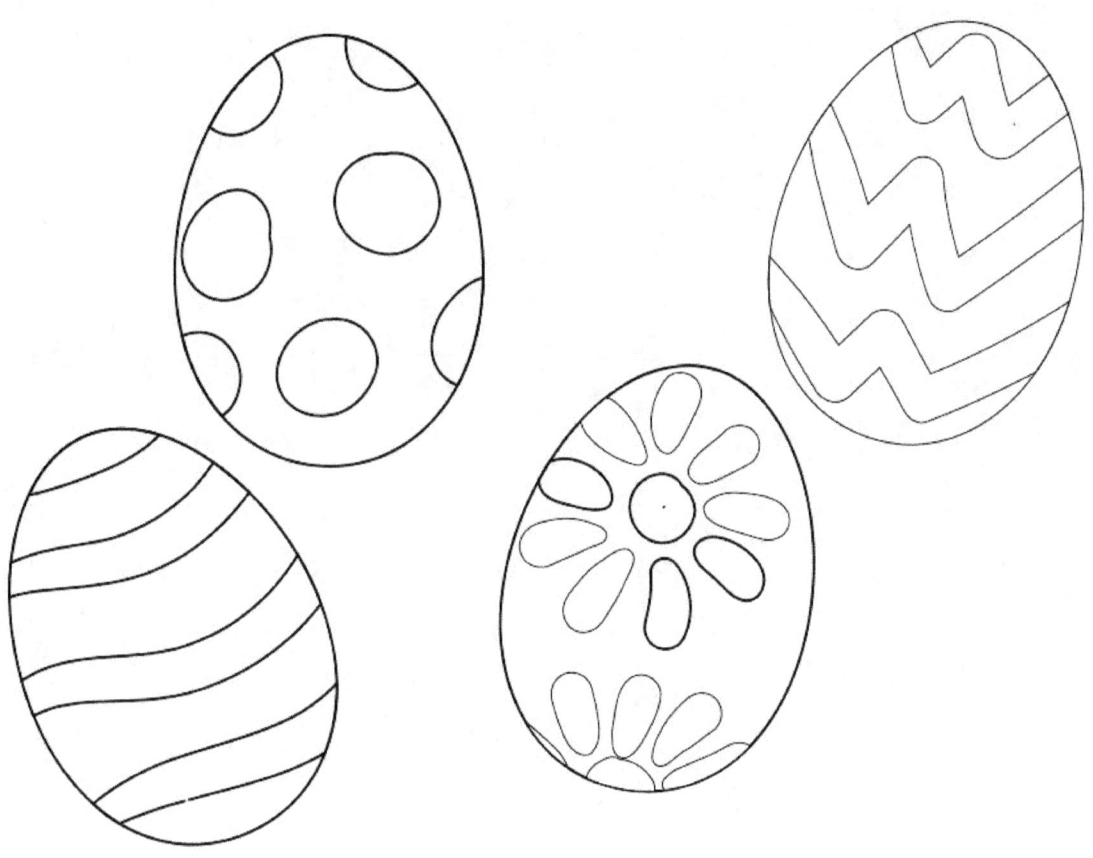

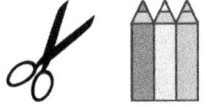

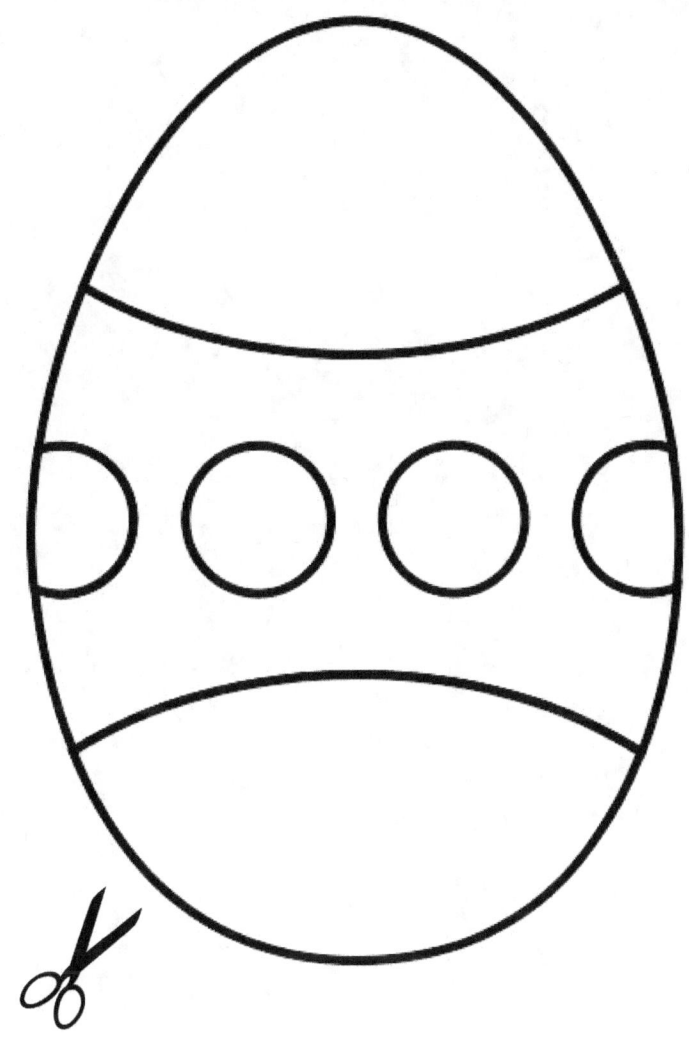

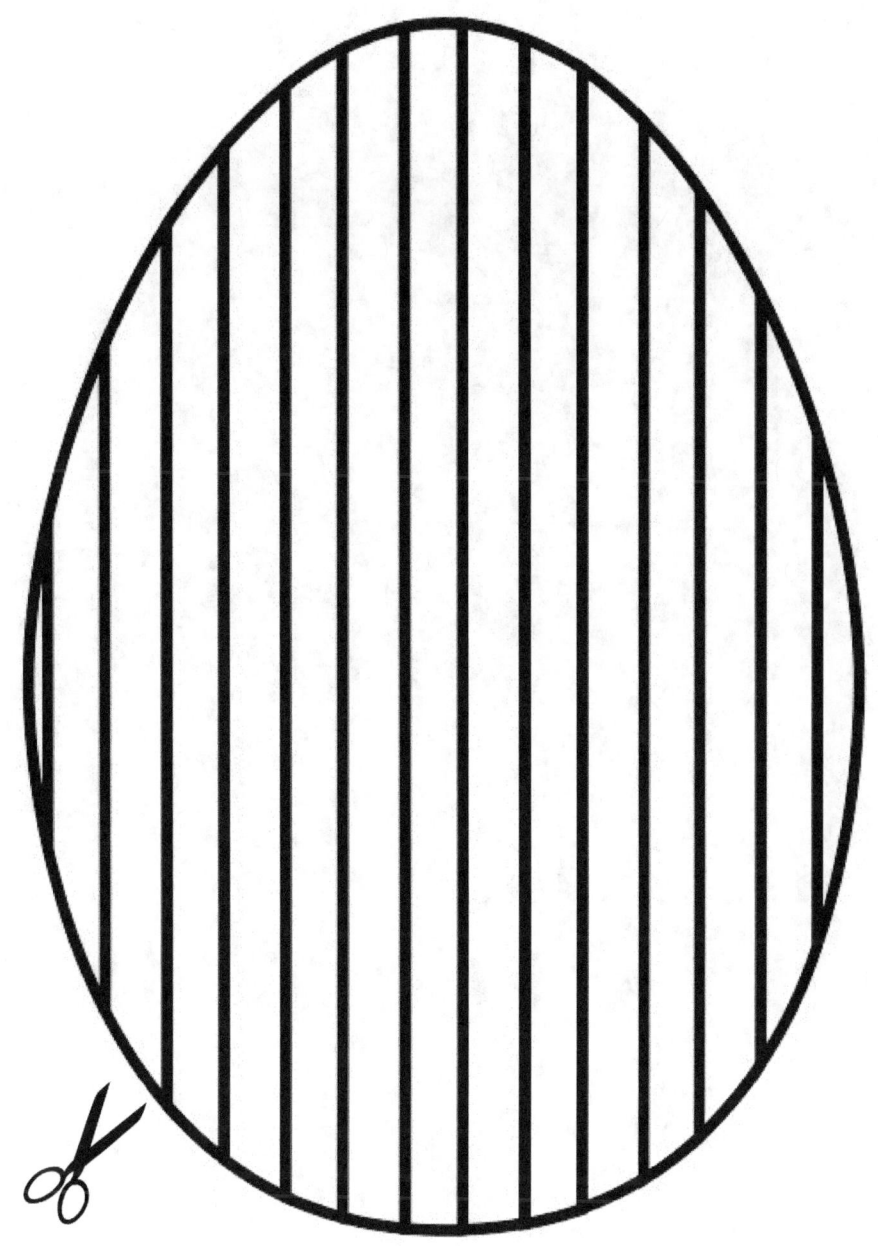

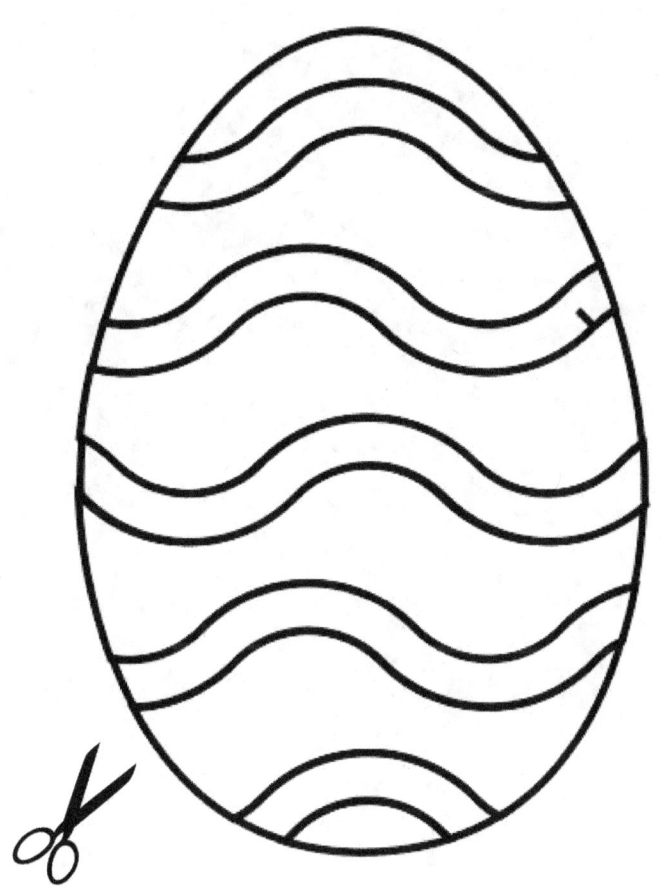

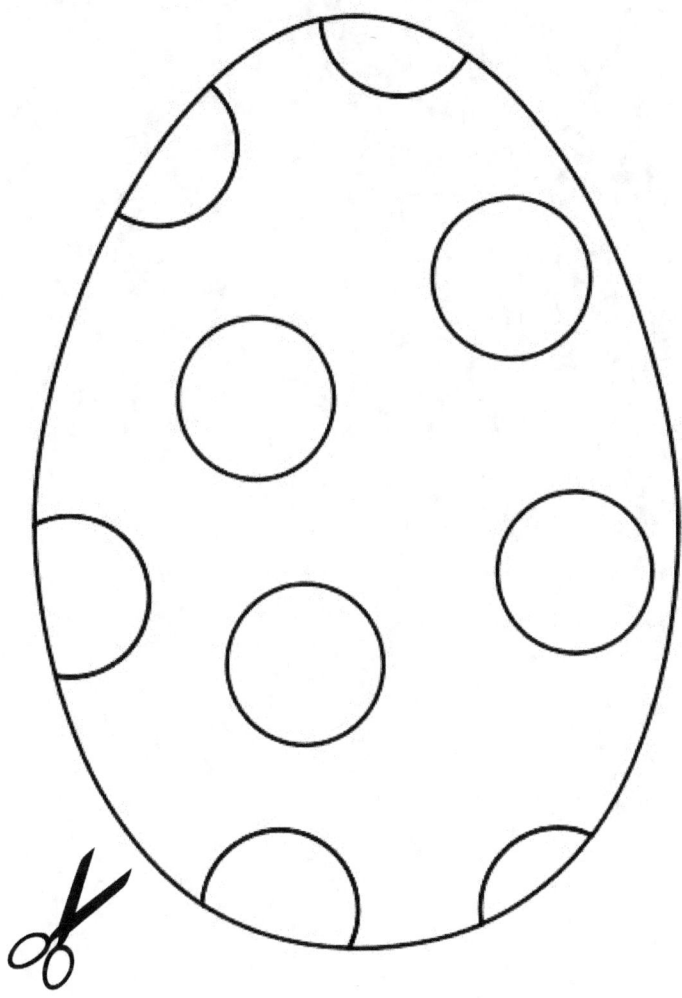

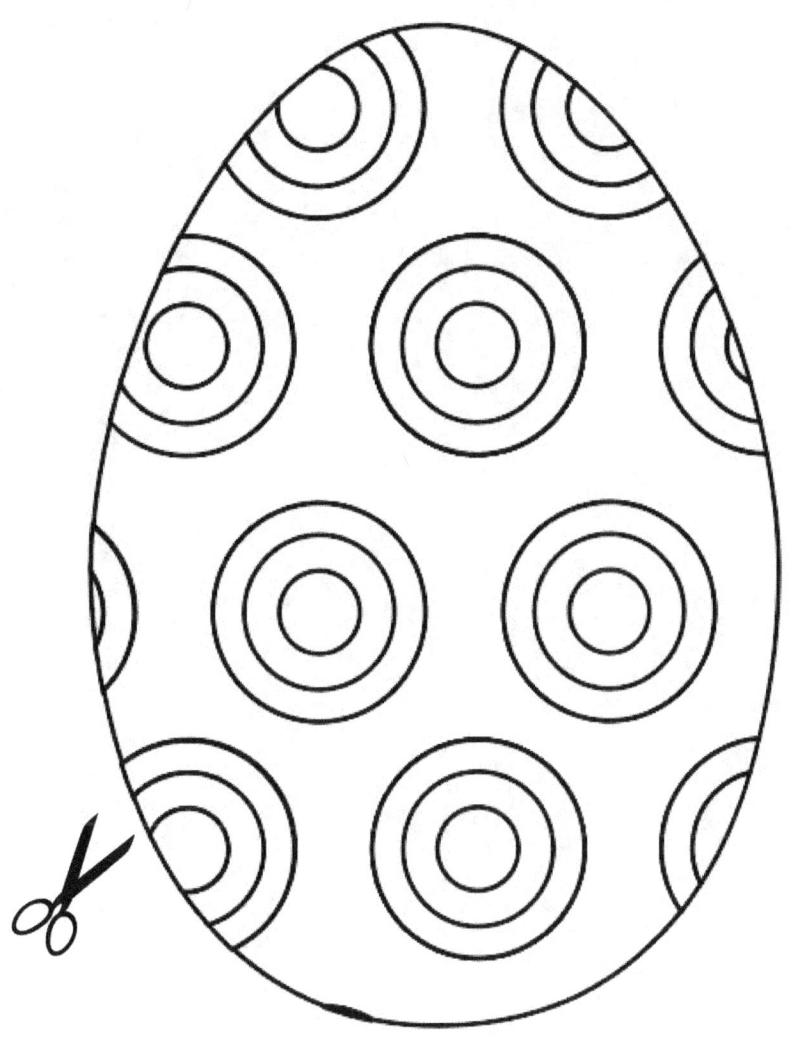

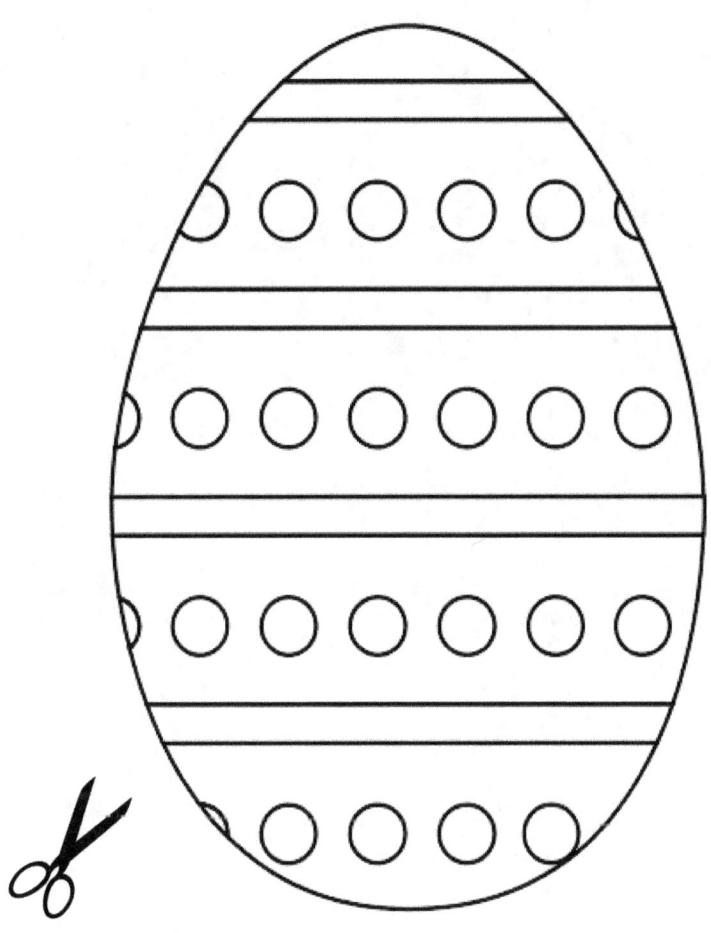

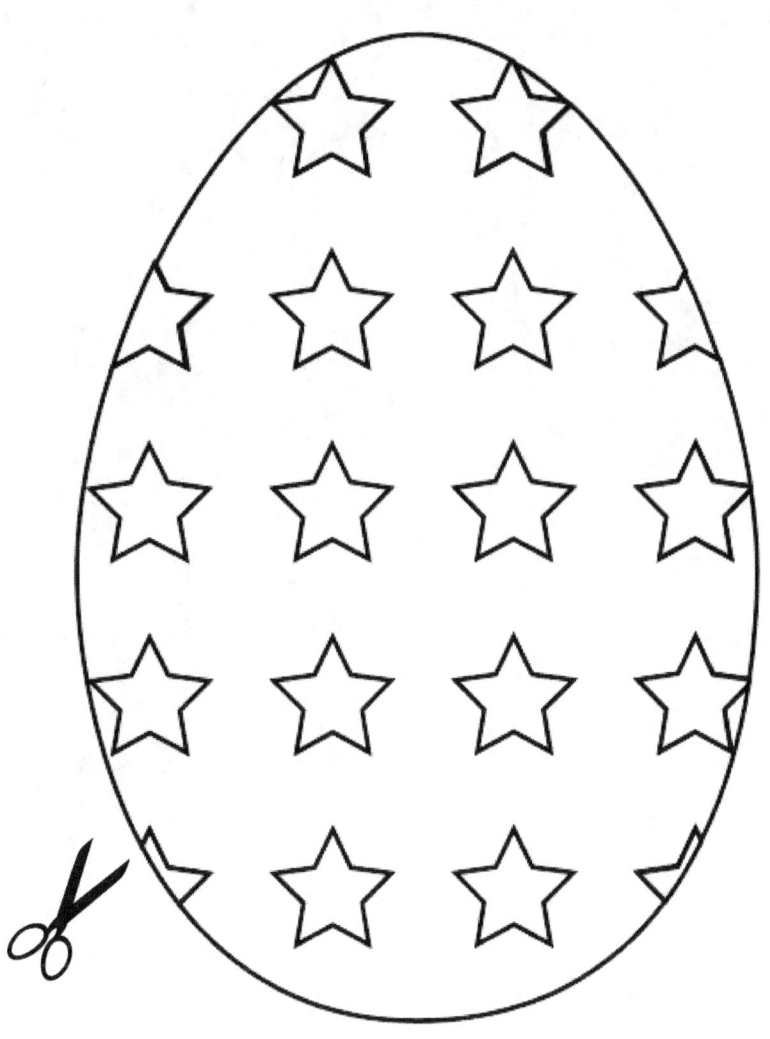

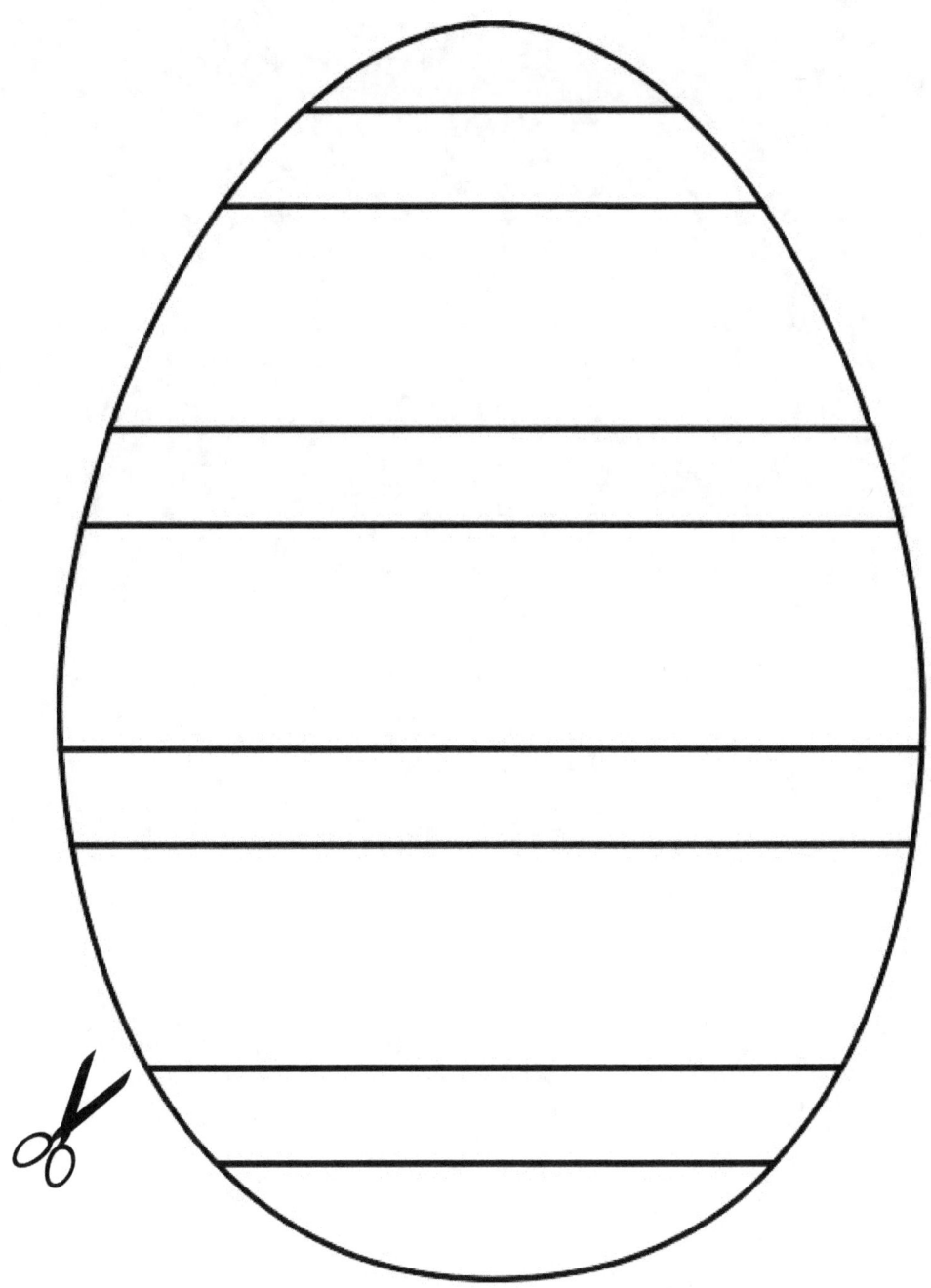

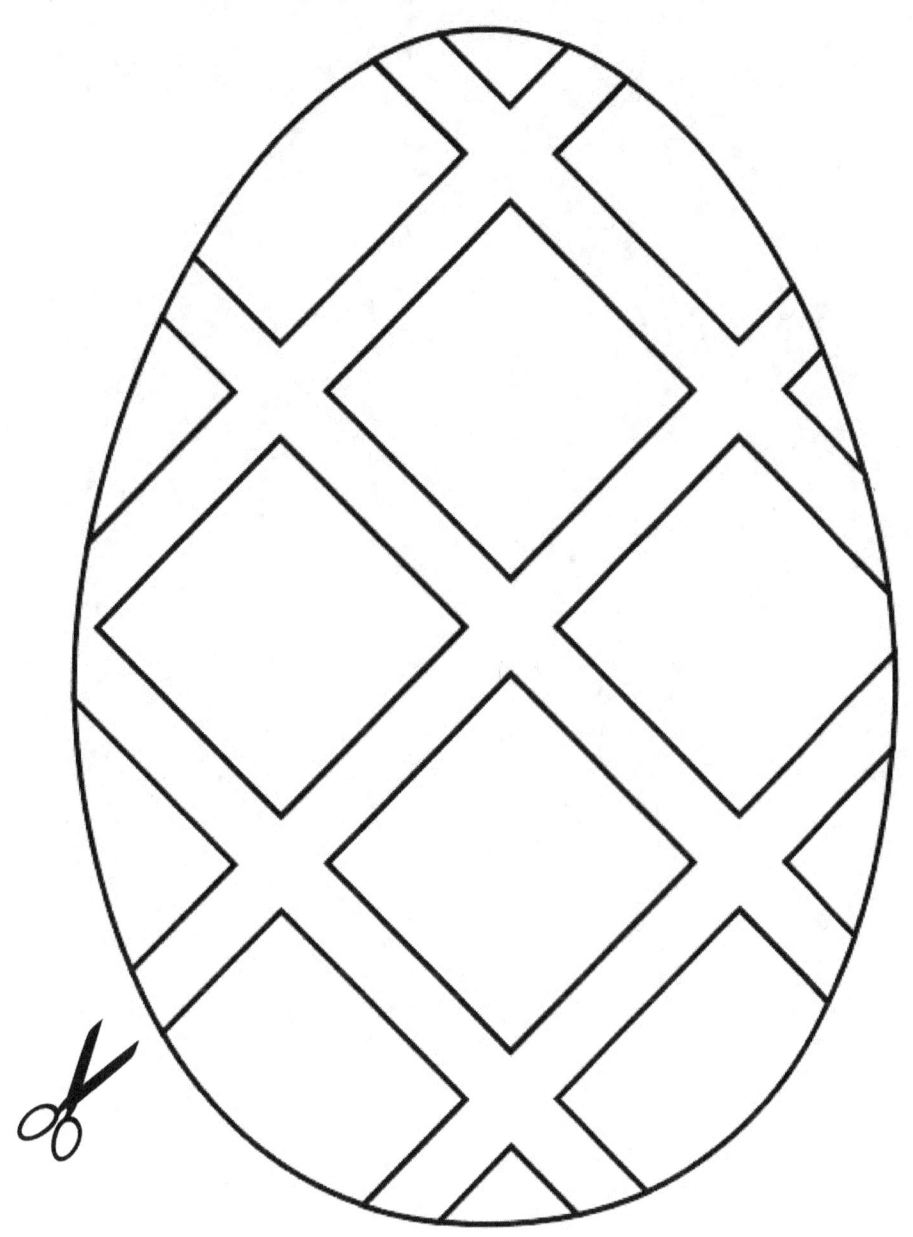

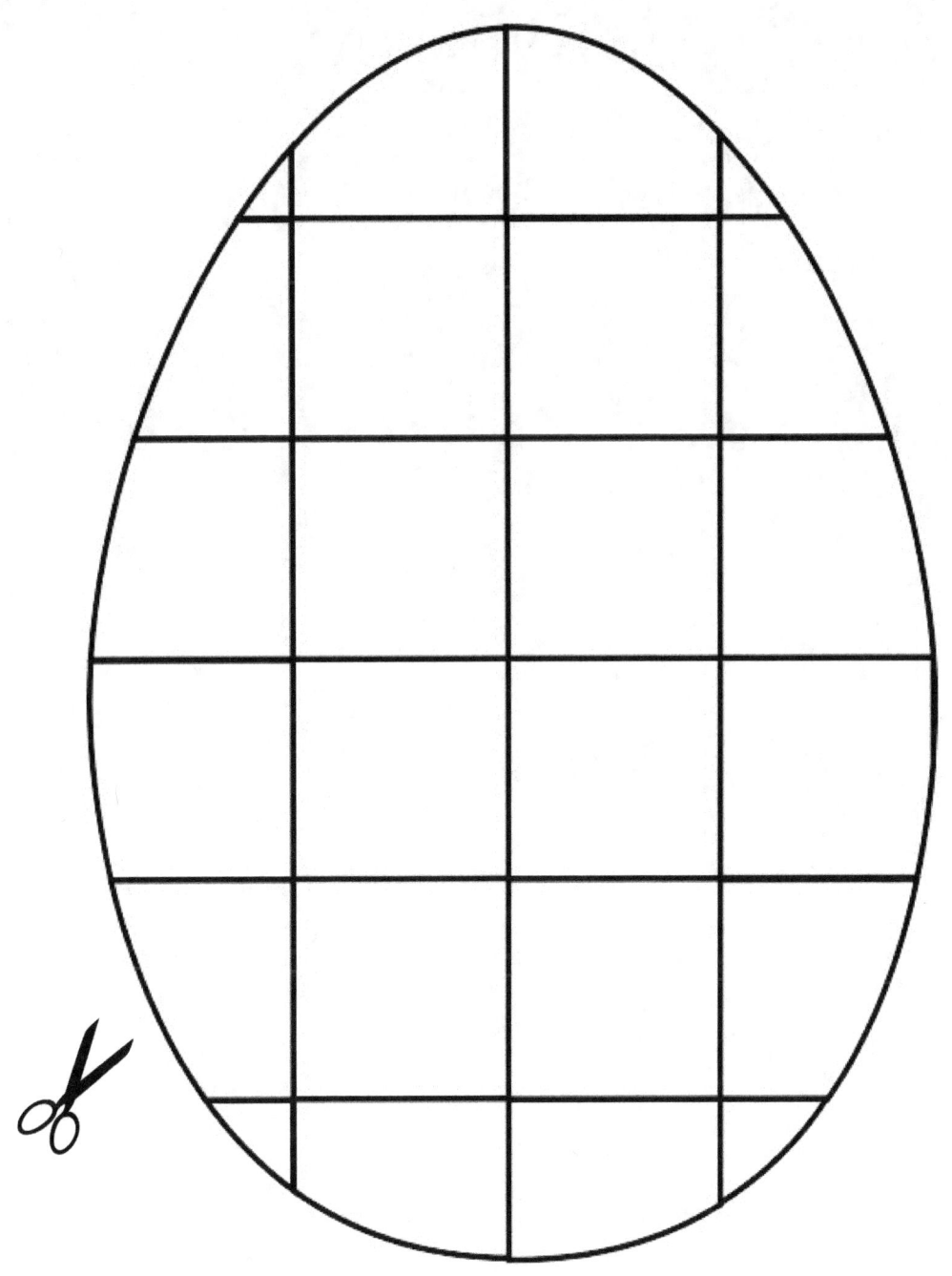

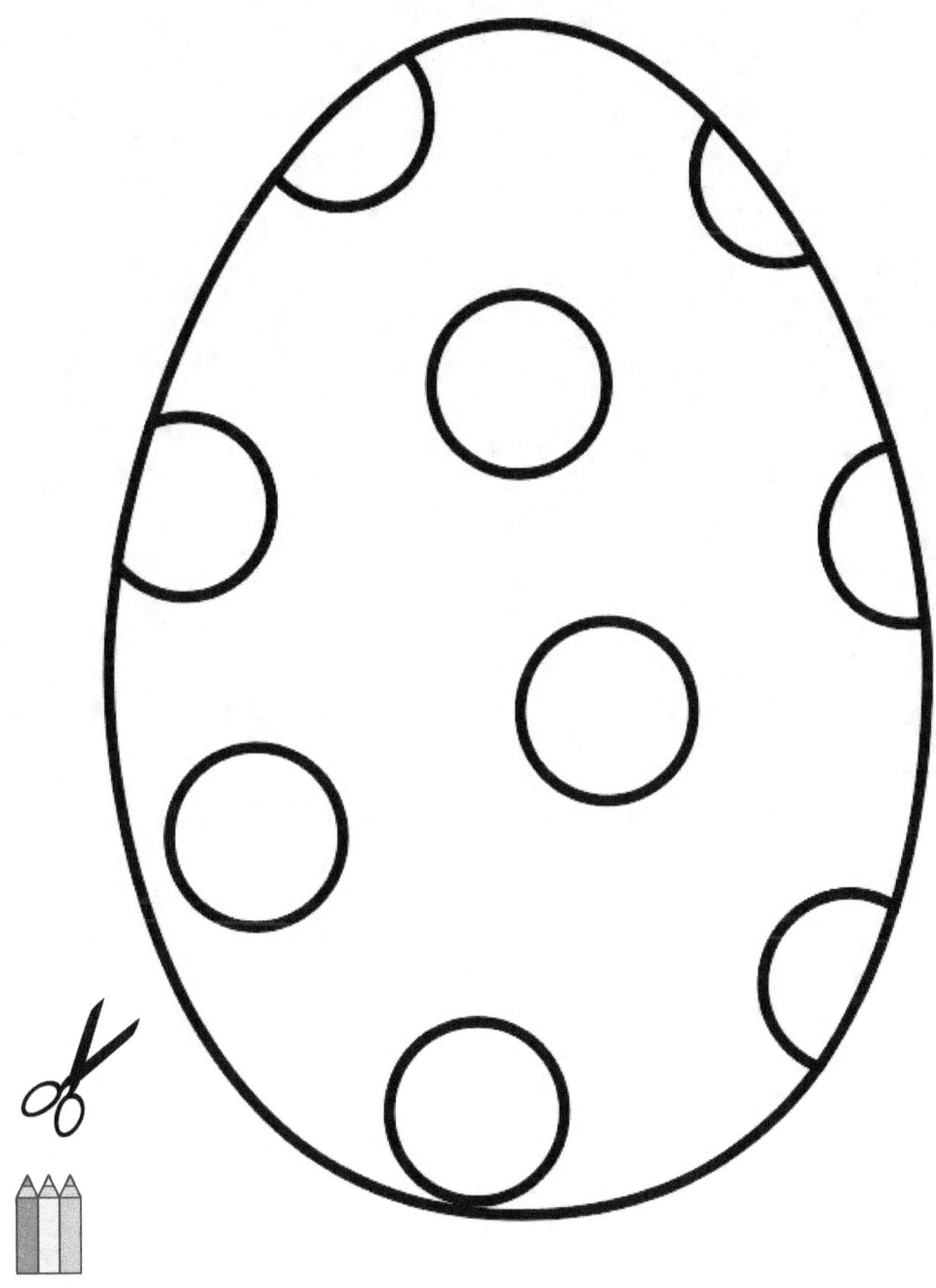

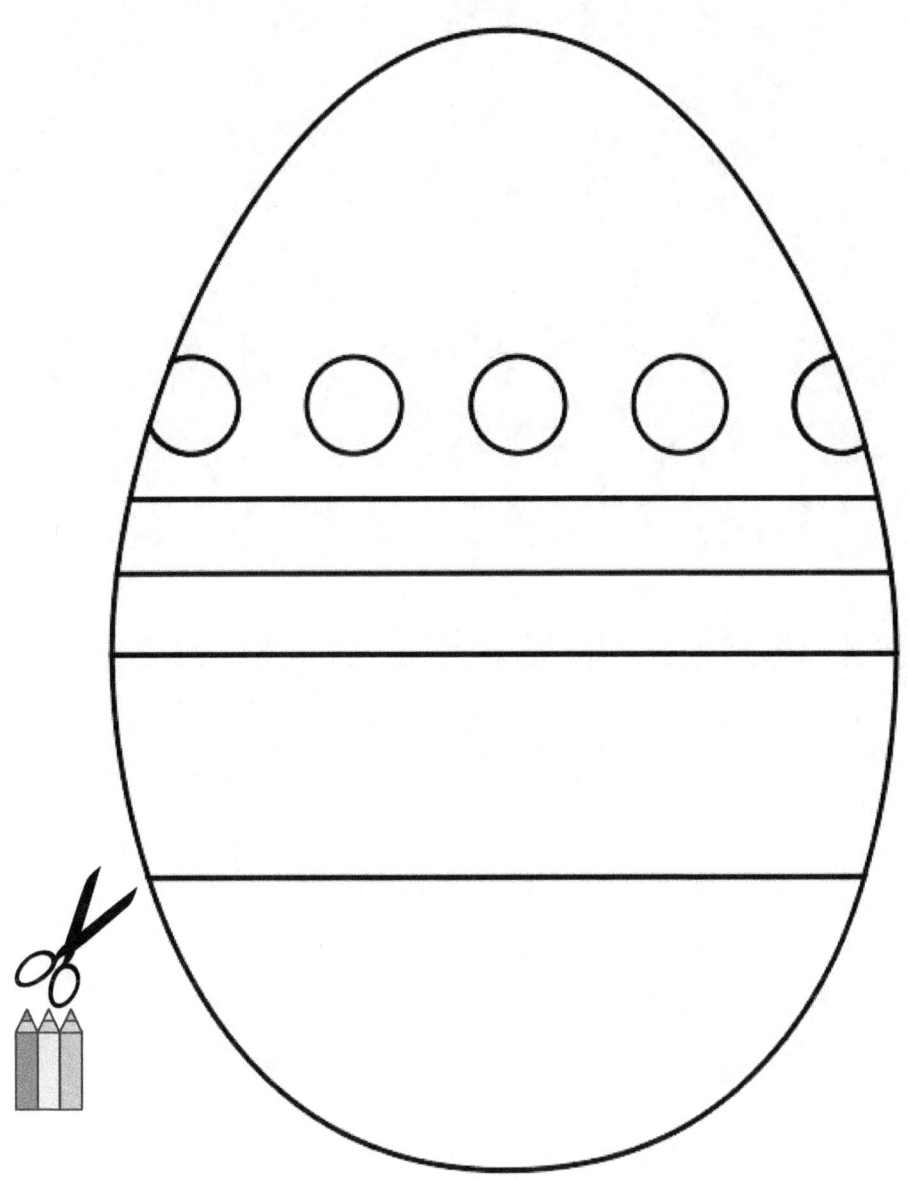

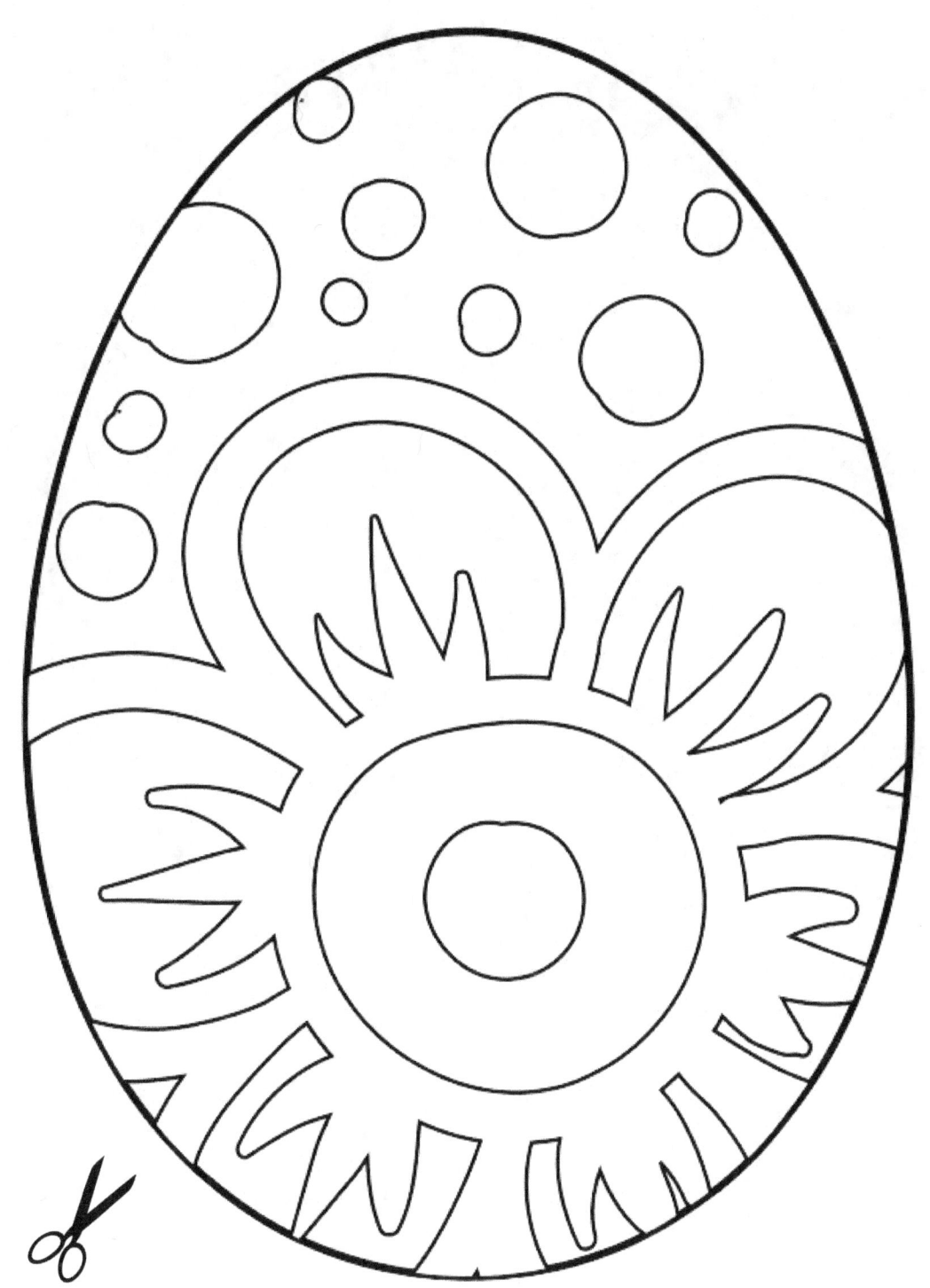

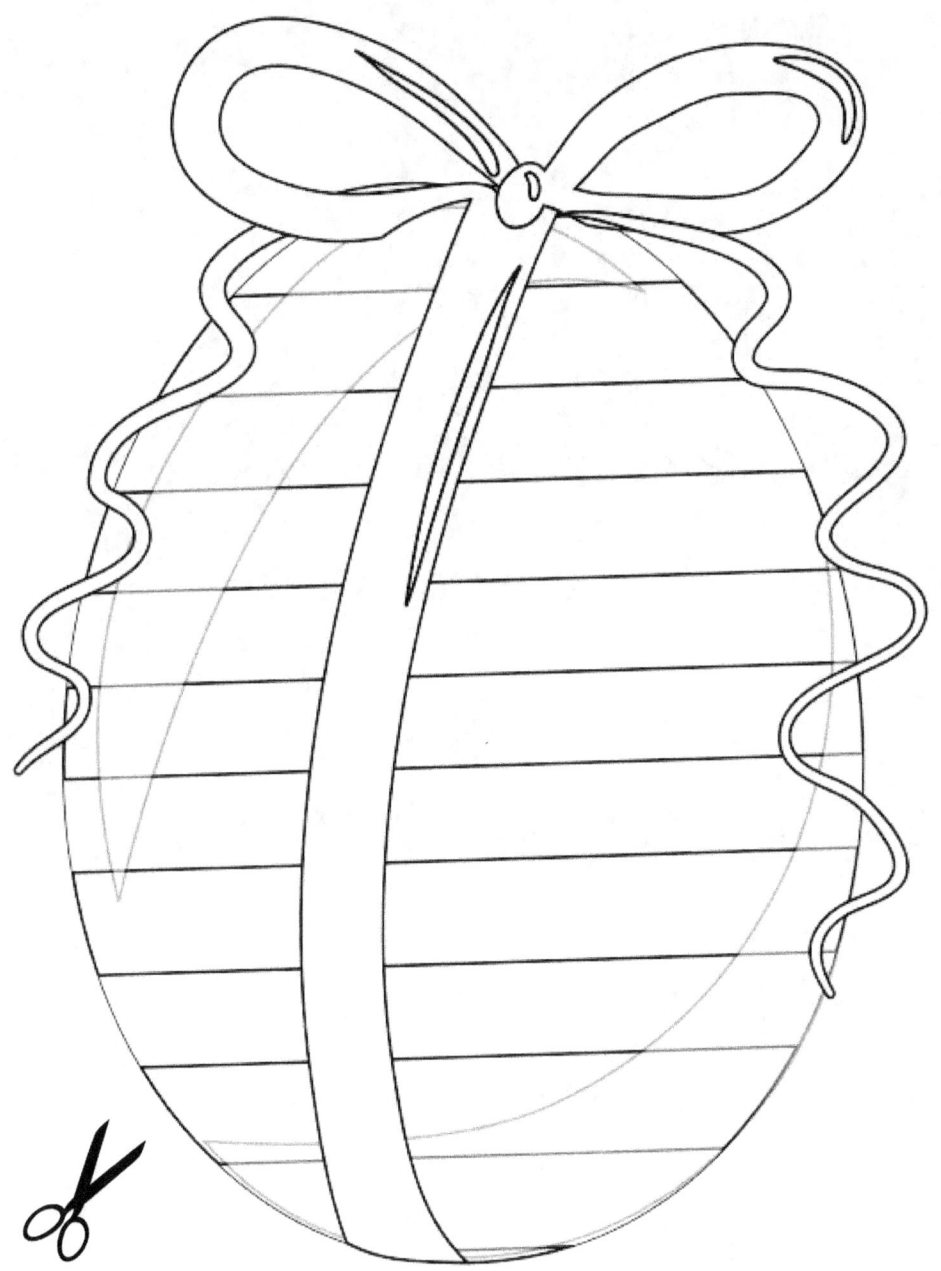

EASTER TIME

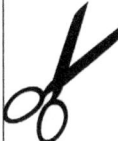

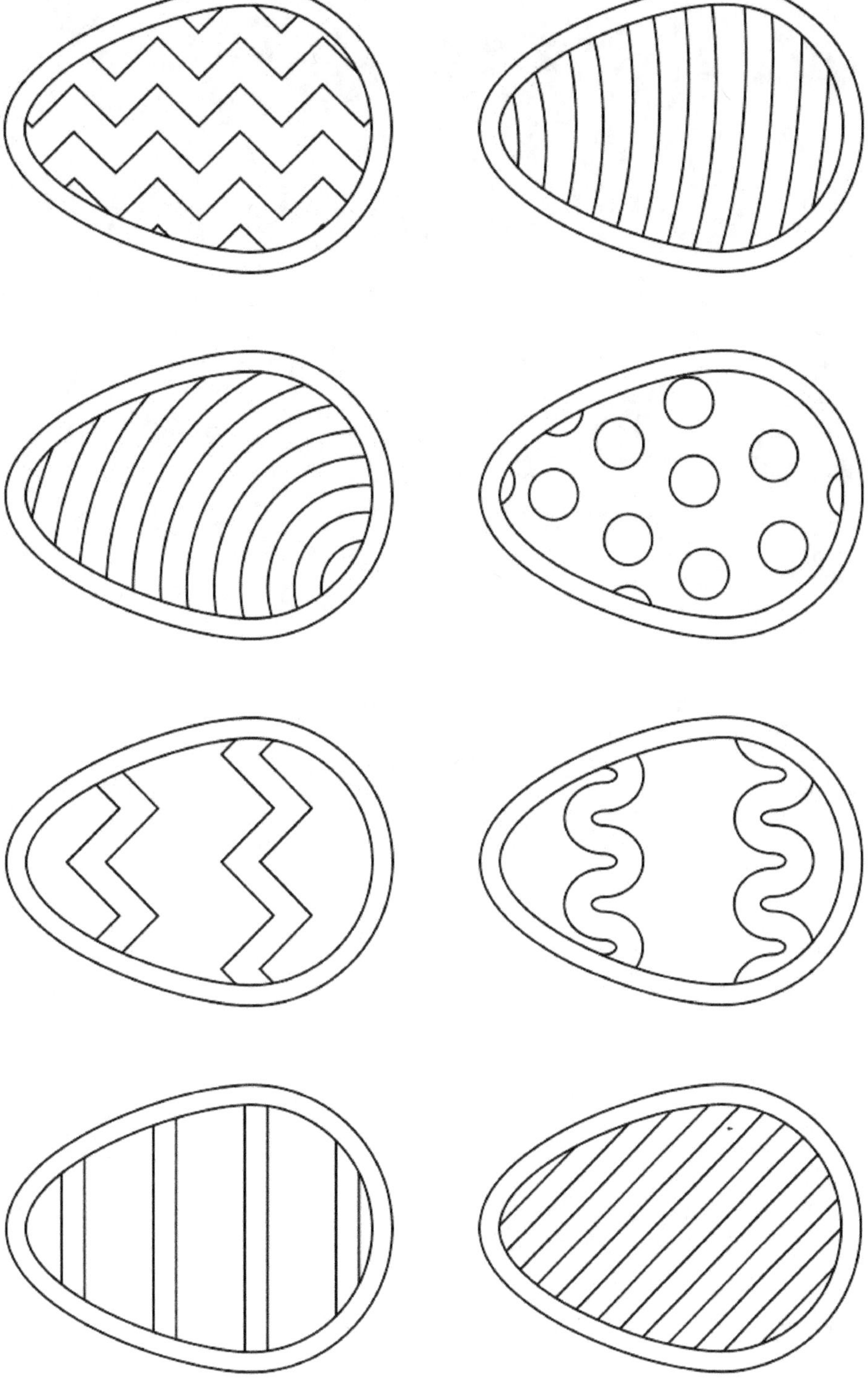

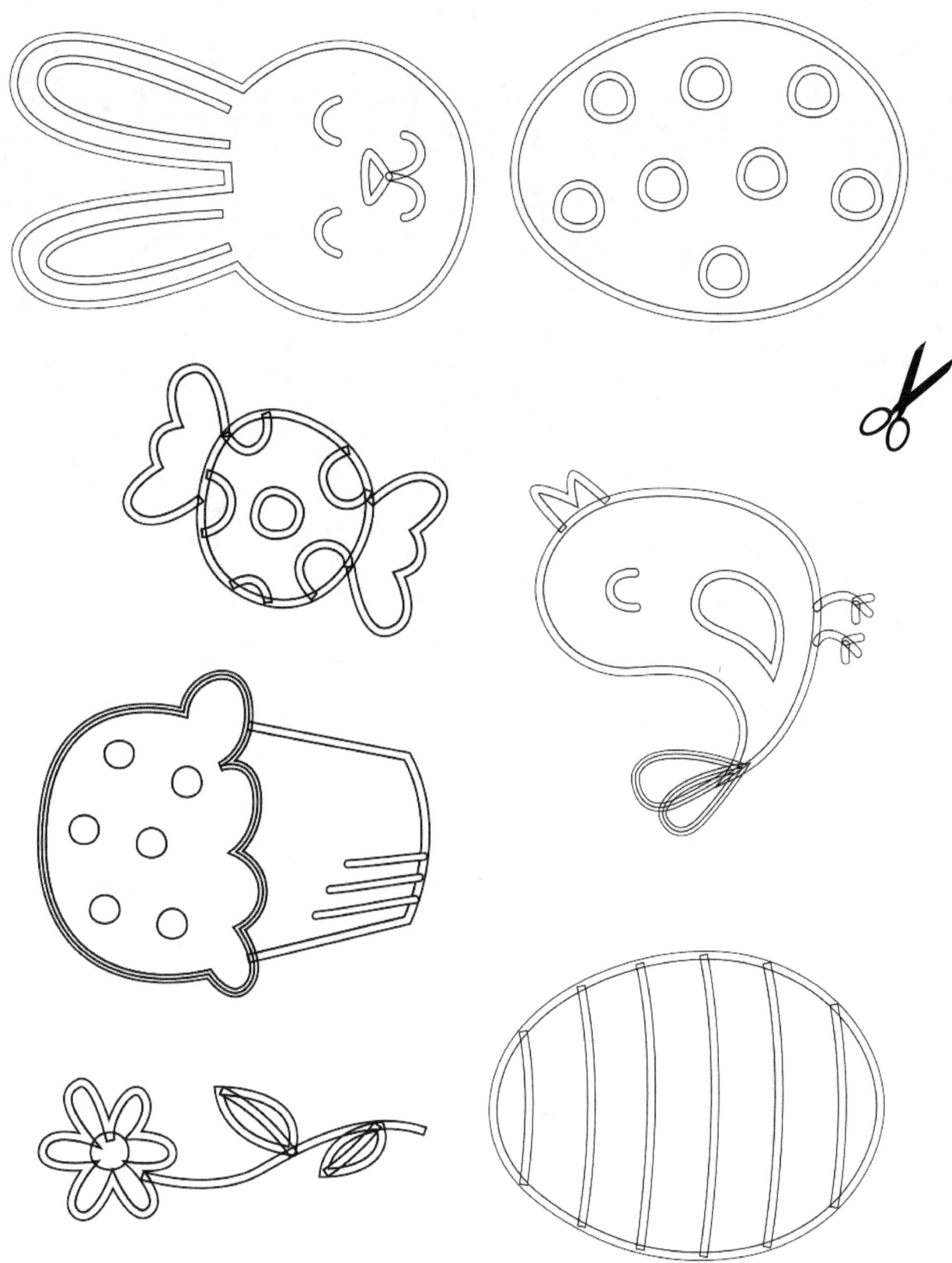

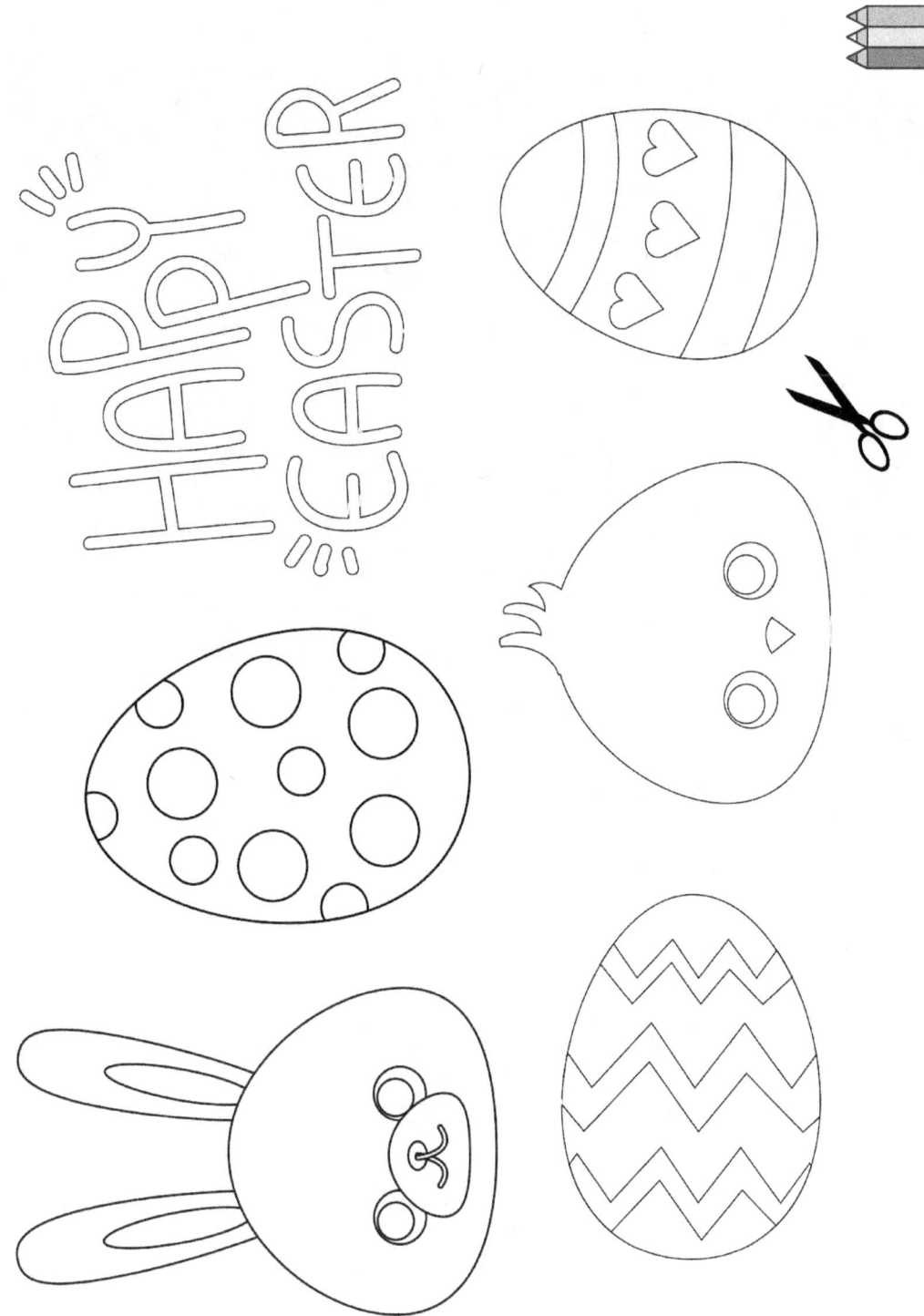

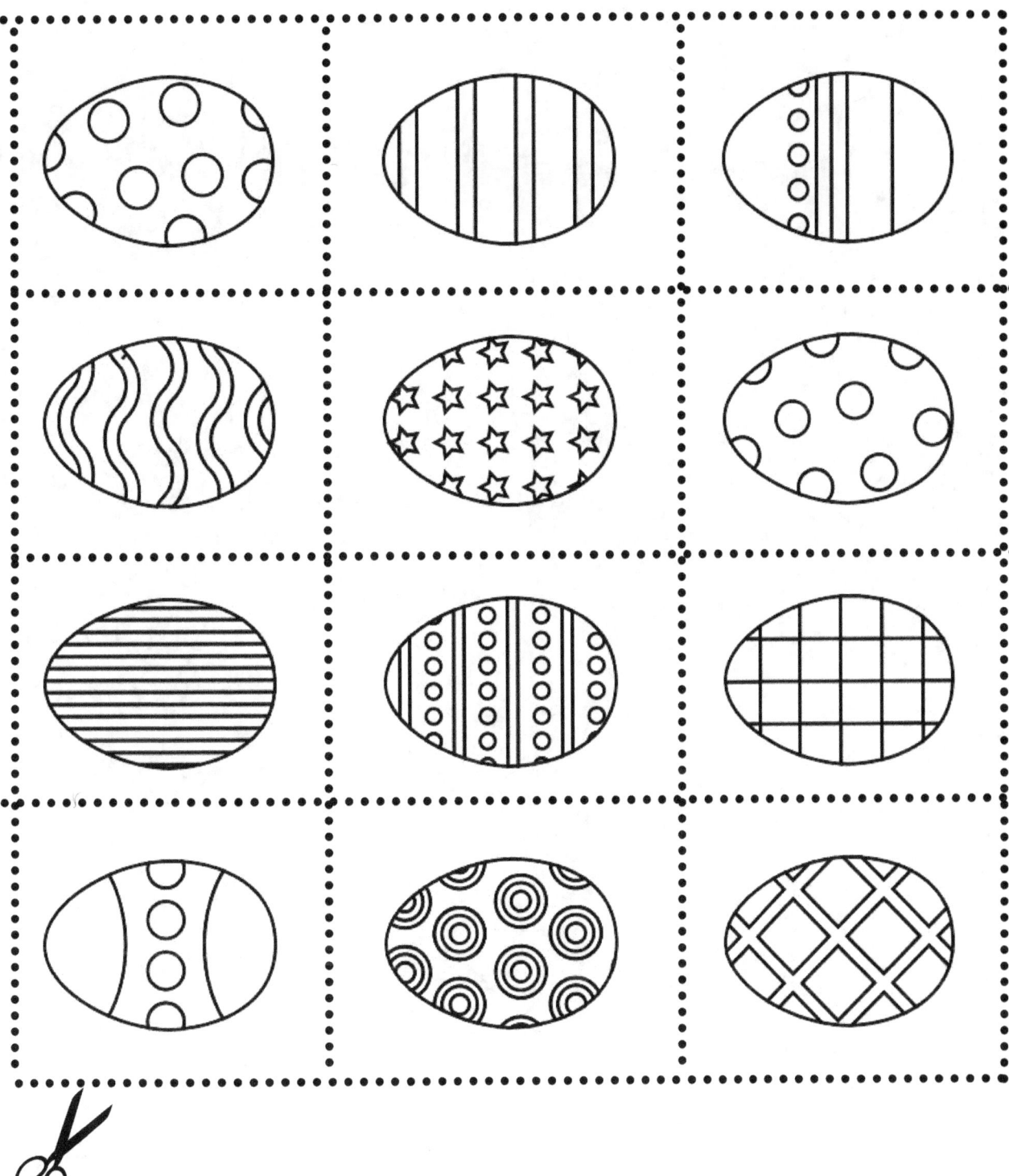

www.ingramcontent.com/pod-product-compliance
Lightning Source LLC
Chambersburg PA
CBHW080900220526
45467CB00008B/2581